AMERICAN PRESIDENTS

Abraham Lincoln

by Rachel Grack

BLASTOFF! 2 READERS

BELLWETHER MEDIA • MINNEAPOLIS, MN

Blastoff! Readers are carefully developed by literacy experts to build reading stamina and move students toward fluency by combining standards-based content with developmentally appropriate text.

Level 1 provides the most support through repetition of high-frequency words, light text, predictable sentence patterns, and strong visual support.

Level 2 offers early readers a bit more challenge through varied sentences, increased text load, and text-supportive special features.

Level 3 advances early-fluent readers toward fluency through increased text load, less reliance on photos, advancing concepts, longer sentences, and more complex special features.

★ **Blastoff! Universe**

Reading Level

Grade K

Grades 1–3

Grade 4

This edition first published in 2022 by Bellwether Media, Inc.

No part of this publication may be reproduced in whole or in part without written permission of the publisher. For information regarding permission, write to Bellwether Media, Inc., Attention: Permissions Department, 6012 Blue Circle Drive, Minnetonka, MN 55343.

Library of Congress Cataloging-in-Publication Data

Names: Koestler-Grack, Rachel A., 1973- author.
Title: Abraham Lincoln / Rachel Grack.
Description: Minneapolis, MN : Bellwether Media, 2022. | Series: Blastoff! Readers: American Presidents | Includes bibliographical references and index. | Audience: Ages 5-8 | Audience: Grades 2-3 | Summary: "Relevant images match informative text in this introduction to Abraham Lincoln. Intended for students in kindergarten through third grade"-- Provided by publisher.
Identifiers: LCCN 2021011377 (print) | LCCN 2021011378 (ebook) | ISBN 9781644875100 (library binding) | ISBN 9781648344787 (paperback) | ISBN 9781648344183 (ebook)
Subjects: LCSH: Lincoln, Abraham, 1809-1865--Juvenile literature. | Presidents--United States--Biography--Juvenile literature. | United States--History--Civil War, 1861-1865--Juvenile literature. | United States--Politics and government--1861-1865--Juvenile literature.
Classification: LCC E457.905 .K64 2022 (print) | LCC E457.905 (ebook) | DDC 973.7092 [B]--dc23
LC record available at https://lccn.loc.gov/2021011377
LC ebook record available at https://lccn.loc.gov/2021011378

Editor: Elizabeth Neuenfeldt   Designer: Josh Brink

Printed in the United States of America, North Mankato, MN.

Table of
Contents

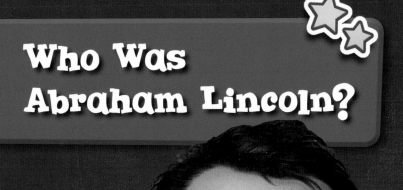

Who Was Abraham Lincoln?

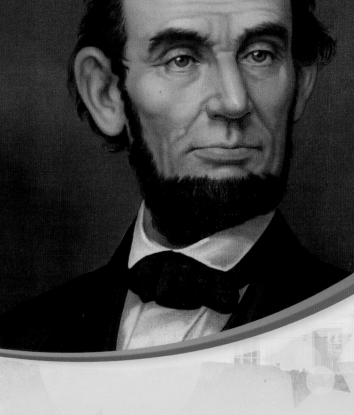

Abraham Lincoln was the 16th president. He led the United States in the **Civil War**.

Abraham stood up for **freedom** for all!

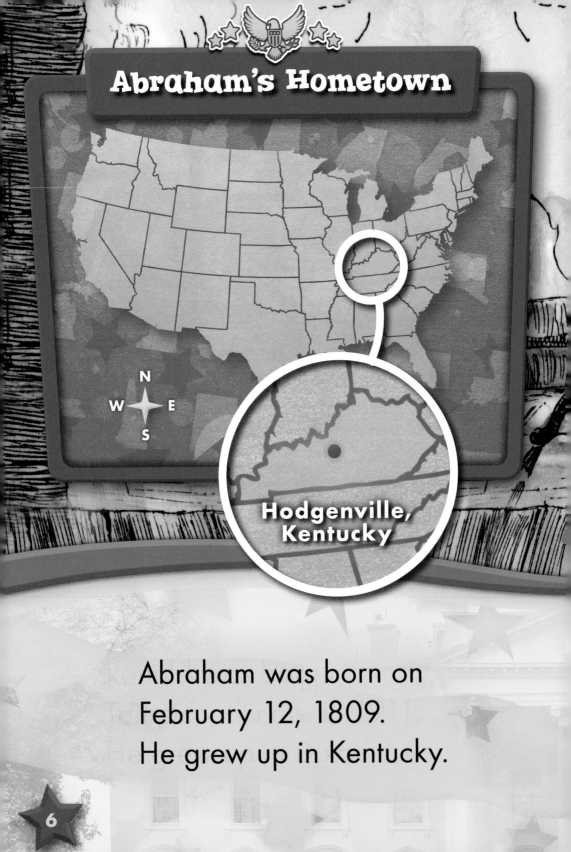

Abraham's Hometown

Hodgenville,
Kentucky

Abraham was born on
February 12, 1809.
He grew up in Kentucky.

He taught himself how
to read. He loved books!

Abraham was a hard worker. He worked many jobs.

In time, he became a **lawyer**. He was fair and honest.

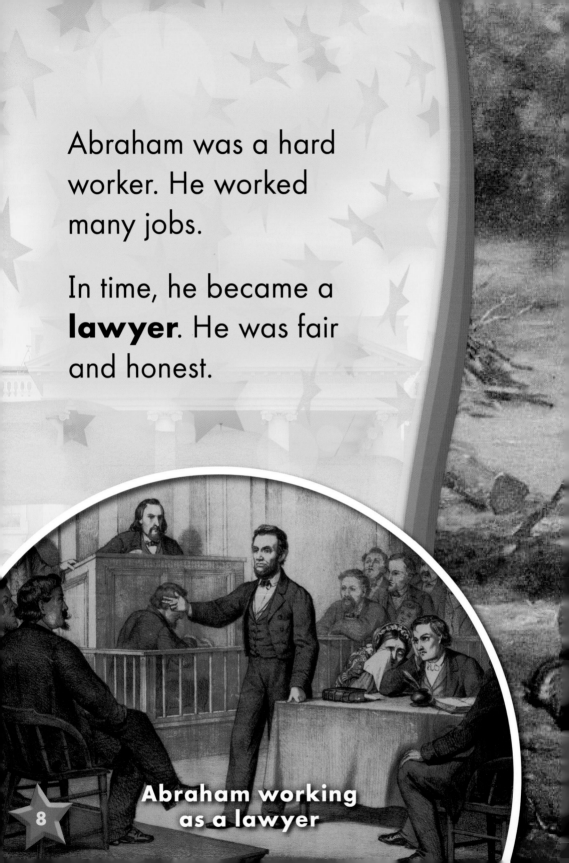

Abraham working as a lawyer

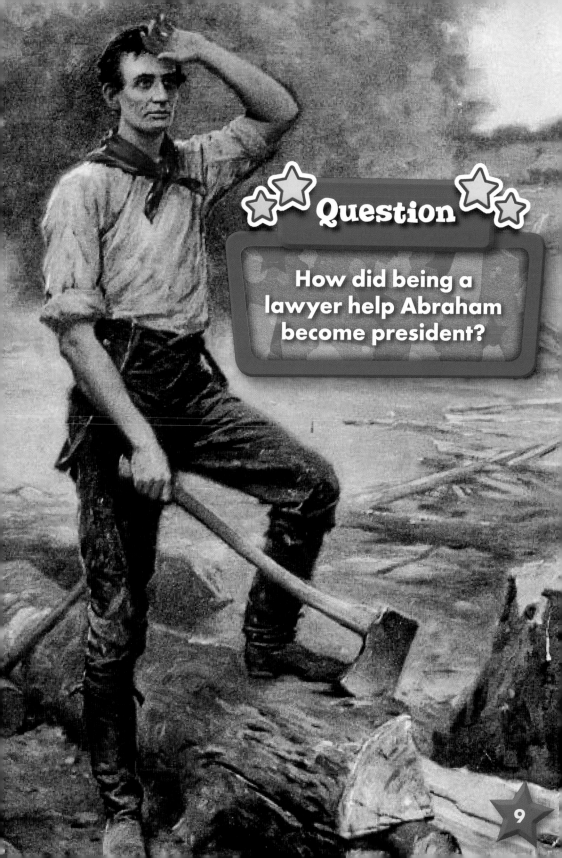

Question

How did being a lawyer help Abraham become president?

9

Abraham worked in the
Illinois **legislature**.
He served for eight years.

Presidential Picks

Books

Robinson Crusoe and
Aesop's Fables

Sport

wrestling

Animal

cat

Music

opera

10

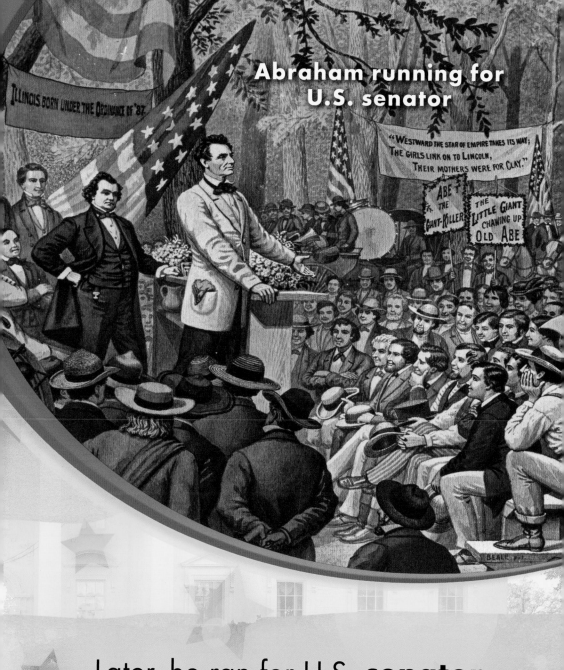

Abraham running for
U.S. senator

Later, he ran for U.S. **senator**.
He lost. But his run made him
more popular!

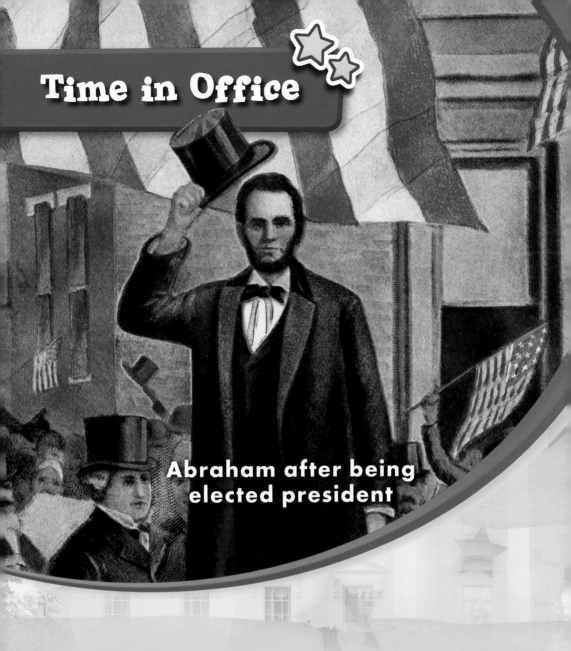

Abraham after being elected president

Abraham was **elected** president in 1860. He wanted to stop **slavery**. Many states agreed with him.

But other states wanted slavery. Seven southern states quickly **seceded** from the U.S.

Presidential Profile

Place of Birth

Hodgenville, Kentucky

Birthday

February 12, 1809

Schooling

self-taught

Term

1861 to 1865

Party

Republican

Signature

Abraham Lincoln

Vice Presidents

Hannibal Hamlin

Andrew Johnson

13

Soon, the Civil War broke out.
It began on April 12, 1861.
Abraham led the Northern states
against the Southern states.

Battle of
Gettysburg, 1863

Battle of Franklin, 1864

There were many bloody battles.

Abraham signing the Emancipation Proclamation

In 1863, Abraham signed the **Emancipation Proclamation**. It said slaves in the South were free. Abraham was reelected in 1864.

Abraham Timeline

April 12, 1861

The Civil War begins

1860

Abraham Lincoln is elected president

January 1, 1863

Abraham signs the Emancipation Proclamation

1864

Abraham is reelected

April 9, 1865

The South surrenders

April 14, 1865

Abraham is shot at Ford's Theatre

April 15, 1865

Abraham dies

The South **surrendered** on April 9, 1865. The war was over!

Five days later, Abraham was shot. He was at Ford's Theatre. He died on April 15.

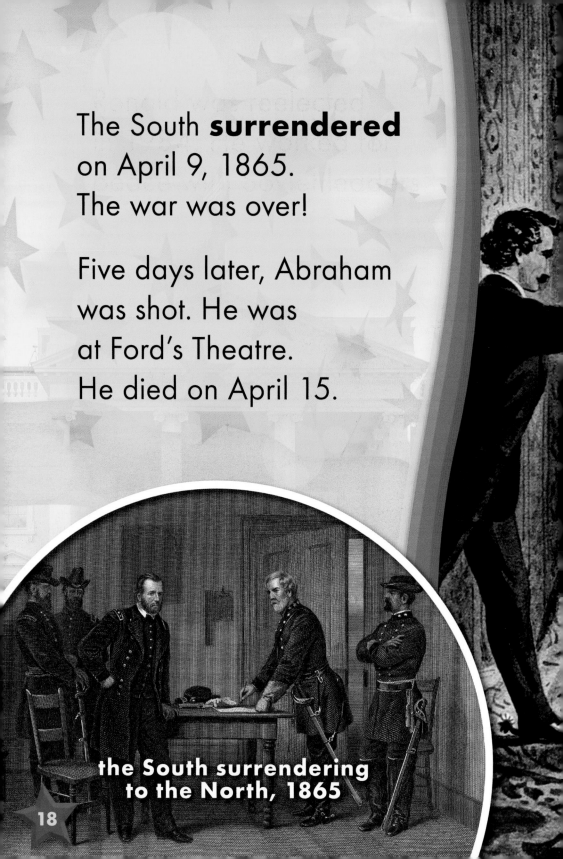

the South surrendering to the North, 1865

What Abraham Left Behind

people celebrating the Thirteenth Amendment being passed

The **Thirteenth Amendment** was passed after Abraham died.

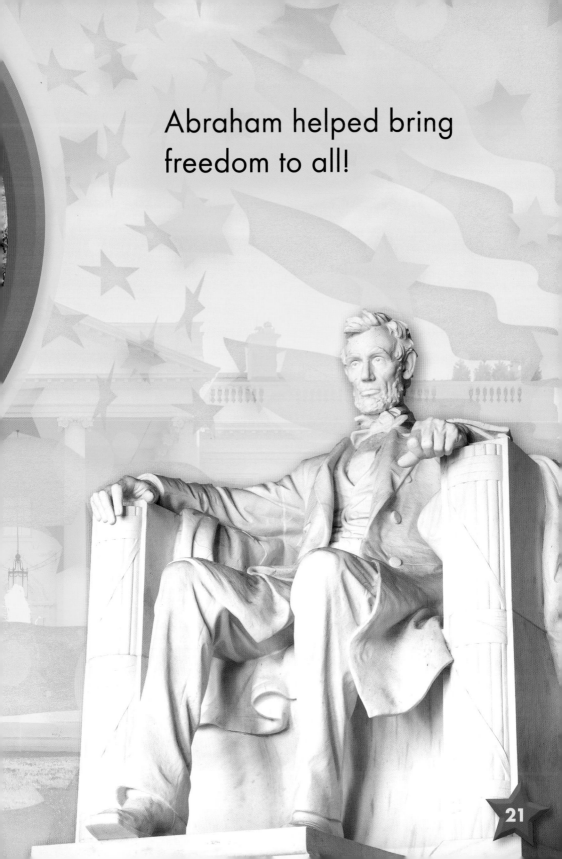

Abraham helped bring freedom to all!

21

Glossary

Civil War—a war between the Northern (Union) and the Southern (Confederate) states that lasted from 1861 to 1865

elected—chosen by voting

Emancipation Proclamation—a document that said all slaves in the South were free

freedom—the right to do and say as you like

lawyer—a person trained to help people with matters relating to the law

legislature—a group of people who have the power to make or change laws for a country or state

seceded—separated from a country and formed a country of their own

senator—a member of the Senate of the U.S. government; the Senate helps make laws.

slavery—the act of owning slaves; slaves are people owned by someone else.

surrendered—gave up and decided to lose

Thirteenth Amendment—the change to the Constitution that made slavery against the law; the Constitution is the highest law of the U.S. government.

To Learn More

AT THE LIBRARY
Dussling, Jennifer. *Long, Tall Lincoln.* New York, N.Y.: HarperCollins Publishers, 2017.

Hally, Ashleigh. *Abraham Lincoln.* New York, N.Y.: AV2 by Weigl, 2018.

Murray, Laura K. *Abraham Lincoln.* North Mankato, Minn.: Capstone, 2020.

ON THE WEB

FACTSURFER

Factsurfer.com gives you a safe, fun way to find more information.

1. Go to www.factsurfer.com.

2. Enter "Abraham Lincoln" into the search box and click ⚲.

3. Select your book cover to see a list of related content.

Index